A B O V E
S E E
L E V E L

1 ABOVE SEE LEVEL

Cover Design: Janiel Escueta

Format: Robyn Norwood Editing™

2 ABOVE SEE LEVEL

Dedication

This book is dedicated to my Daddy God, the orchestrator of my life, for being a God who keeps His promises and continuously blesses me in spite of.

To my Mom, who desired the very best for me and my four siblings and proved it by living her life in perpetual motion. Her physical health was challenged often, but her mental health was strong enough to bear the burden. During one of her many hospital stayovers; she listened as I critiqued this manifesting list of quotes. With her infinite wisdom and relaxed voice tone, she shared her thoughts on one of my now favorite quotes. "Marriage is not ruined from the outside." My Mom said "some things should be sacred". We agreed. Her life on earth expired January 10, 2016. To my dad, John.

To my daughter Jordan and granddaughter LaRae' Denise, my son Kenneth, daughter in-law Keosha and grandson, Messiah. To my siblings: Puddin, Baby Sister, Mickey and Tinker who will be forever known by their nicknames.   I love you for all that you are and all that you hope to become.

Acknowledgements

This book could not have been written without the value of words that was instilled in my life at an early age by two of my best educators.

Thank you to:

My Mom, an avid reader, for surrounding us with books and dictionaries;

My Aunt Daisy, a school teacher, for being a stickler for pronunciation and the placement of words. She wanted to hear the 's' and the 't' and the l, m, n, o, p, s';

My family and friends, for enduring countless hours of conversations; my mentee, Bailey Poll for cataloging and sorting my first set of registered quotes; Regina Breeze for editing the manuscript prior to publishing; and to everyone for paying attention to my words!

Introduction

This book of quotes was birthed from a rolodex of life lessons. There is no irony in the manifestation of my life...from the moment I was conceived, the knitting of my body to my spirit with the framework hidden...my thoughts were there. The grandmother of a dear friend said, "you never know who you are raising".   "Before I formed you in the womb I knew you, before you were born I set you apart...Jeremiah 4:5.

These captured moments of learning were recognized when I became erudite that God set me apart and created me to pay attention. He not only created me to pay attention to my attention, but to use my attention to help others pay attention to Him. Without a doubt, I have missed many opportunities by not being attentive and even misused my attention by paying it to the wrong people and useless things.

I am unsure of the exact instance in time when I realized that paying attention was advantageous. Growing up I distinctly do recall funny remarks, perplexing references, disengaging comments and unexplained actions made by adults. I was smart enough to know that I could not ask questions to gain understanding; yet keen enough to pay attention to what seemed to be a story line. At times, I paid attention for sheer entertainment and collected mounds of information with nowhere to store them except in my innermost thoughts.

I am hilariously inclined to think that my fervor to talk is attributed to me paying attention, listening but being limited with what I could really say aloud. My uncle would speak often of my gift of gab. I thought it was simply my ability to repeat what I heard and learned. All in all, none of this was an indicator of what God had set me apart to do. I use this funny story during the opening of many presentations: When I was growing up, my mom would offer to pay me to stop talking; a nickel to stop talking, a dime to stop talking and sit still. When neither of the two bribes worked, she would offer me a quarter just to stop talking to her. One day, when I was older, I asked her "where is all my money?" She said, "You never stopped talking to earn any."

"Pay attention to your attention"

On another occasion, I wanted to get permission from my Mom for my sister and I to go out to play. Receiving permission to go anywhere was like getting a bill passed in Congress. Unlike the House of Congress; which has separate committees and officers, my Mom was both. I rehearsed the question in my mind, then out loud; careful to use "may we" instead of "can we", not speaking too fast, pausing where air commas should be and even clearing my throat. Now, down the hallway to the kitchen, where Mom spent most of her time. Before reaching her, I was fully convinced that I had the right statement formatted in my head to receive a positive response. As I am walking, I am practicing my sentence structure. After a number of renditions, I begin to repeat the final one aloud. "I'm going to say…Mom may we go to", and before I could complete my perfect rendition of the question, my Mom replied, "I'm going to say no." Instantly, I was frozen in my tracks and learned one of my greatest lessons;

"Be careful what you say aloud, unless you are ready to be heard."

We have witnessed someone make the mistake of speaking out of turn, divulging an idea not well thought through, or simply not yielding to the temptation to spew out exactly what is on their mind in the moment. Nonetheless, if you are not ready to be heard, be careful what you say aloud.

I have intentionally assembled these words for the purpose of sharing and teaching lessons, but most importantly to stimulate the mind and massage the heart.

ABOVE SEE LEVEL

LINDA PROCTOR-MERRITT

"The first time we encounter a lesson; may not be the same time we learn the lesson." ~ lproctorm

There are instances when we are present but yet not engaged. Our lack of engagement, regardless of the reason will allow the experience and the lesson to escape. We are all guilty of assuming that because a person is present it guarantees learning. Imagine, if this were the case; a child that has been riding in the backseat of the car and experienced the trips to the grocery store has learned how to drive and shop for grocery.

"One's perception is one's truth…ONE TRUTH." ~ lproctorm

It is without argument that what a person perceives is their truth. It is unfortunate when their ONE truth disallows them to intellectualize the possibility of any other truth. "People will say 'it's all good' to label a time when there is more to be desired, but perhaps not worth the effort to seek clarification. This non-applicable phrase will rob us of resolution. When things are running smoothly, the situation `silently defines itself as, 'it's all good'. Subsequently, when something occurs that is less than desirable, it is cavalierly enveloped and sealed with "it's all good". The envelope will be unsealed when you least expect!

"Just when you think it's over...it's the beginning." ~ lproctorm

We cheer about the last hour of the work day, the first day of the weekend and just when we think it's over, another hour or day is beginning.

Time is too short

to cheer away...even on a long day. ~ lproctorm

"Trying to teach something that you have not learned is like giving away something you have not earned."

~ lproctorm

"Patience has no statute of limitation." ~ lproctorm

Can you recall hearing someone say "I have been patient long enough"? What is long enough?

Patience is a virtue because it extends life to others.

> Proverbs 14:29
>
> Whoever is patient has great understanding, but one who is quick-tempered displays folly.

"Kindly speak into your life the way you expect others to." ~ lproctorm

We expect others to speak to us better than we speak into ourselves. We need kind words, gentleness, patience and understanding. You owe it to yourself to be your own best friend.   This means you are responsible for how you make you feel!

When was the last time you said a kind word to yourself?

"Fault Does Not Fix It!" ~ lproctorm

We will make mistakes and sometimes
it will be your fault.

- Blaming
- Justifying
- Minimizing
- Denying

...only makes things worse.

Accepting fault increases the possibility of
reaching a resolution.

Knowing who's at Fault it is not enough to
Fix IT.

"Wise men know the rules. Wiser men know the exceptions." ~ *Iproctorm*

"Make room for clarity and it will make room for resolutions." ~ *lproctorm*

"It is unfair to hold others accountable for what we cannot resolve within ourselves"

"Be willing to be wrong." ~ lproctorm

Wrong certainly has its negative connotation and it doesn't' feel good. Imagine being wrong and feeling good about it or being right and wishing you were wrong.

If you have not experienced it, look forward to the time;

- When you hope you are wrong.

- When being wrong challenges you to grow.

- When being wrong relieves your heartache.

- When being wrong encourages you to be humble!

.

"**M**otivation is for a moment;

Inspiration is for a lifetime."

~ *Iproctorm*

21 ABOVE SEE LEVEL

"In matters involving the heart –
Play
Checkers...

Crown people often. Otherwise,
Play Chess." ~ lproctorm

Goal of the Game:

Checkers: crown a man and make him King; which gives
him power.

Chess: checkmate the King. This threatens his power.

"Another form of intimacy is listening with your heart." ~lproctorm

Try it. Your Heart

will become cheerful!

"Be careful who you let change the best of you before you meet the person who deserves and appreciates it." ~ *lproctorm*

"Dating is an intentional opportunity to make new memories together."   ~lproctorm

"Kissing is a wonderful language, not spoken enough. It is sharing common thoughts silently." ~ lproctorm

"18 years will feel like a life
sentence if there is no love it."

~ Iproctorm

"A cold shower is
less regretful!"

27 ABOVE SEE LEVEL

"Give PREP talks instead of PEP
talks, PREParation goes further."

~ lproctorm

"We are often in one's company,
but not always in their presence."

~ lproctorm

"Depend on your inner GPS. God's Positioning System." *~ lproctorm*

- ☐ Your GPS may take you directly to your destination.
- ☐ Your GPS may take you the scenic route.
- ☐ Your GPS may continuously reroute you.

"Promise your spirit a safe and happy place…keep your promise."

~ lproctorm

31 ABOVE SEE LEVEL

"If you pick up too much in your mind and heart, allow your hands to carry it...*Pray*." ~ *lproctorm*

"Imagine not believing.   It is impossible   to   imagine without believing." ~ *Iproctorm*

Do you believe this?

33 ABOVE SEE LEVEL

"Fight fair or the fight is never worth it." ~ lproctorm

"We may not be able to orchestrate order, but choose not to be the confusion." ~ *lproctorm*

"There is more than one way to
earn trust, but only way to lose it."

~ lproctorm

"It is unfair to hold someone responsible for your silent thoughts." Silent thoughts are our dangerous assumptions." ~ *lproctorm*

"The same reason someone may love you, can be the same reason they dislike you." *~ lproctorm*

"Hire the optimist not the genius."

~ lproctorm

"Only share your story with those who <u>deserve</u> to hear it." ~ *Iproctorm*

"If we cannot ask for help without self-judgement, we do not accept help without judgement." ~ *lproctorm*

Awareness: "The thing that changed you in that moment."

~ lproctorm `

Dysfunction: "The moment you recognize you can no longer function with that thing."

A dysfunctional moment: A husband and wife made an agreement to establish a budget to live on. The husband was the overseer of the account and the wife certainly had access.

The husband said he was placing the money in the front door with a teaspoon and the wife was using a back hoe to take it out of the back door.

The wife is writing checks from the back of the checkbook as if they were going to clear without the husband noticing.

"Some things are taught. Some things are caught." ~ *lproctorm*

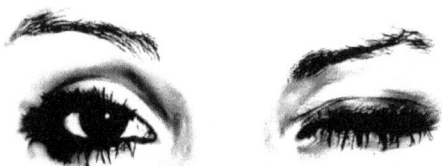

43 ABOVE SEE LEVEL

"If *you* want to know about me, ask me to complete an application. **If** *you* want to know me...listen!"

~ *lproctorm*

"**ATTITUDE** is more

valuable than ability."

~lproctorm

45 ABOVE SEE LEVEL

"To earn the right for others to express their vulnerabilities, I too must become vulnerable." *~ lproctorm*

"Don't think twice, twice."
~ lproctorm

This means you START and END with the same thought.

"Everything in nature sings.

Enjoy the beautiful music!"

~ lproctorm

"Love is as <u>powerful</u> as it is <u>painful</u>."

~ lproctorm

"Disobedience.

Disaster.

Deliverance. In that order." ~ lproctorm

Obedience is better than sacrifice and to heed is better than the fat of Rams.

I Samuel 15: 22 NLV

"Your body sometimes wants what your heart does not need!"
~lproctorm

51 ABOVE SEE LEVEL

"Living from the inside out or the outside in? This is the question."

~ lproctorm

What is the answer?

A: _____

"Are you like everyone or anyone?"

~ *Iproctorm*

53 ABOVE SEE LEVEL

"When you think the answer is
  NO...know **God** has something
  better."

~ lproctorm

"It is dangerous for me to think more of myself; however, it is equally as dangerous to think less of what God thinks of me." ~ lproctorm

"Your WILL must be stronger than your resistance!"

POWER

"Your discipline must be stronger than your WILL!" ~ lproctorm

"Baggage creates bad
relationships, not bad people."
~ *lproctorm*

How is your baggage packed?

"Don't make excuses for yourself and not be willing to excuse others... That's discrimination."

~ lproctorm

"Wherever there is an offense, there is a debt. Pay up, apologize....and do it quickly!" ~ lproctorm

"Forgiveness feels better to the forgiver than the forgiven."

" *Manners* are not just for strangers and new friends!" ~ lproctorm

"Words can be measured…If not, they could not weigh heavily on the heart." ~ *lproctorm*

"Four things you cannot recover: **the stone after the throw**, the word after it's said, **the occasion after it's missed**, time after it's gone, LIFE after it has expired." ~ lproctorm

"Some relationships should change and some should end." ~ *lproctorm*

"We CANNOT grow and fall alone...nor should we want to"
~ lproctorm

"The moment you are in is the only time guaranteed!" *~ lproctorm*

65 ABOVE SEE LEVEL

"There are some thoughts you cannot avoid and some feelings you cannot deny." *~ lproctorm*

Be true to yourself.

"Be led by your spirit and escorted by your feelings." ~ lproctorm

Our spirit is our gut instinct - it never lies. If we allow our emotional thinking to make decisions, we might SEE that we have been misled...

"Great relationships have elements of surprise & risk!" ~ lproctorm

Enjoy them both.

MY PERSONAL MANIFESTO

When I am old, I want to look back and know I...

- CREATED JOY
- LIVED AUTHENTICALLY
- WAS COMPASSIONATE
- WALKED LIGHTLY
- GAVE GRACE
- POOLED MY RESOURCES
- VALUED THE POWER OF LOVE
- SHARED MY EXPERIENCES

~ lproctorm

"Is it possible for a ONE night stand to stand more than ONE night?"

~ lproctorm

"Things rarely go wrong, they *simply* change."

~ *lproctorm*

"Learn the Art of <u>WHEN</u>.

When extracts fundamental and supplementary
information.   It is a call to action."

"Learn the Art of <u>YES</u>."

Yes gives an affirmation to execute the action.

~ lproctorm

"Live fully and your encounters will be your reminders." ~ *lproctorm*

"Being insidious is sneaky."

Simply say what you really mean! ~ *lproctorm*

"If the only tool we have is a hammer, everything will look like a nail. Think with an assorted tool belt."

~ lproctorm

- Think Positive
- Think Optimistic
- Think Twice
- Think outside of the box
- Think Big
- Think Above SEE Level

"Marriage is not ruined from the outside." *~ lproctorm*

My mom always said "some things should be sacred". Outsiders should not have the privilege to that sacred place.

I remember going to a house warming party of a newly married couple; the home was fabulous! Beautifully

decorated rooms, astounding window treatments, themed bonus rooms, breath taking views, the chef's kitchen with double sub-zero refrigerators, huge patio overlooking an endless pool, marble floors, inset televisions, bathrooms to live in and walk-in closets you could run in. Then the tour ended...

"Our bedroom is "sacred" and off limits!"

"There is a moment in life where everything wrong can be right. – LIVE FOR IT!" ~ lproctorm

How many times have we exchanged words or thoughts with someone and the underlying statement is...if you had just...or if I had only...? In those moments it could have been right.

"Do you know the difference between your circle and your audience?" ~ lproctorm

- Your circle is camped around you. Your audience sits in front of you.
- Your circle gives you energy.
- Your audience needs your energy.
- Your circle embraces you.
- Your audience applauds you.

"I desire to be married and have a human man hold my hand while he prays!" ~ lproctorm

God promised me the desires of my heart. -Psalms 37:4

"What comes from the heart speaks to the heart." ~ *Iproctorm*

"**NEVER** is a frightening word."

~ lproctorm

81 ABOVE SEE LEVEL

"Don't misuse your energy covering up pain; instead...expose the pain and use the energy to recover from it." *~ lproctorm*

82 ABOVE SEE LEVEL

"Be Truthful and Honest...there is a difference." ~ lproctorm

A wife was having an affair and, after a moment of passion, she realized that a passion mark had been left on her neck. She became nervous about how to explain the mark to her husband.

To avoid telling the truth about the passion mark, she burned her neck with the curling iron. When she was asked by her husband what happened to her neck, she quickly replied "I burned my neck with the curling iron.

Truthful or Honest?

"Challenge poor thinking." ~ *lproctorm*

"When you are unsure what to say...Use this filter:"

~ lproctorm

Is it true?

Is it necessary?

Is it kind?

Does it serve someone's best interest?

85 ABOVE SEE LEVEL

"Wealth is having more money than time. Broke is a mindset."

~ lproctorm

5 Tips to Generate Income

Use your:

EDUCATION

SKILLS

TALENTS

PASSION

CONNECTIONS

"When you were born the world rejoiced and you cried."

Live your life so that when you die the world cries and you rejoice!"

WRITE YOUR EULOGY HERE

"Raise your children like they are
   little people. They soon grow into
   big people." ~ lproctorm

"Do all the good you can, by all the means you can, in all the ways you can, in all the places you can, at all the times you can, to all the people you can, as long as ever you can."

-John Wesley

"Do it NOW!"

–Linda Proctor-Merritt

"Yes We Can!"

-President Barack Obama
Date of Birth: August 4, 1961

44th President of the United States of America
2008-2016

91 ABOVE SEE LEVEL

"When was the last time your heart smiled? Don't live then die with an unhappy heart." ~ *lproctorm*

"Expose the darkness to <u>your</u> light."

~ lproctorm

Let your light shine before man, that they may see your good works, and glorify your Father which is in Heaven.
-Matthew 5:16

"Dig deep to find your source then use it as a resource." *~ lproctorm*

"Don't exchange your glass half empty thoughts for an empty glass."
~ lproctorm

There will be times when we must run our thoughts by someone else to get an additional perspective, to have our thought challenged and/or stretched. In these times, select someone who can offer you what you need and not someone with less insight.

"**Persistence** not Perfection!" ~ lproctorm

Persistent people perfect processes which appears
like perfection.

"Learn the difference between understand and agree." ~ lproctorm

Understanding is the ability to comprehend, but does not mean agree. We spend a surmountable amount of time in unrelenting conversations, where the simple difference is; understand and/or agree.

"Channel optimism by embracing optimistic words."

"Make

LOVE

visible."

"**[**Set boundaries**]** – it reduces the
fear of being vulnerable."

~ lproctorm

"Choices shape your life."

The **BIG**.

The small

The Frequent. The Frequent!   *~ lproctorm*

101 ABOVE SEE LEVEL

"I'm too nice."

No such thing.

~ lproctorm

People feel like they are too nice when they give more
than they should, to someone
they should not, hoping the same someone will
recognize their giving and be nice in return.

"Make a decision. Make a change."

~ lproctorm

103 ABOVE SEE LEVEL

"Achievement depends on you!

Success depends on who likes you."

~ *lproctorm*

"People learn best when they believe in you; not when they need you."

~ lproctorm

The human need is such a state that the choice to learn in that moment is driven by whether the information will satisfy the need. If it does not, the necessity to learning is minimal.

"Looking for a sponsor? God sponsors inspired people!" "You never have to deny what you do not say."

~ lproctorm

Don't be reckless with the tongue that has the power to speak life and death.

"Worrying _today_ does not cure _tomorrow's_ problems." ~ lproctorm

Therefore; do not worry about tomorrow for tomorrow will worry about itself. Each day has enough trouble of its own.

-Matthew 6:34

"Our thoughts can be backed by so much insecurity, that it creates lies we believe....and tell others."

~ lproctorm

"Everything is easier said…when no one is listening." ~ *lproctorm*

"We are naturally judgmental; it's evident in the way we ask and answer questions!" *~ lproctorm*

"We let people who care nothing about us; control the most important part of us!"

~ lproctorm

"EXPECT THE EXPECTED!"

"We are conditioned to expect the unexpected…"

~ lproctorm

"THERE IS <u>NO</u> BURDEN OF MY

PAST THAT WEIGHS MORE

THAN THE PROMISES OF MY FUTURE."

~ lproctorm

113 ABOVE SEE LEVEL

"People do not change overnight, but one night may make a difference!" *~ lproctorm*

"PEACE transcends intellect.
Be still long enough to notice."
~ *Iproctorm*

"Be willing to listen."

The least that can happen is you hear something you already know; however, the MOST that can happen is you learn something you did not know.

"You may not always get the things you want, as fast as you want, as much as you want, the way you want or even when you want. BUT when you do, it makes wanting worth it!" ~ *lproctorm*

"IMPOSSIBLE...I'm possible." *~ Iproctorm*

"Who you choose to surround yourself with is who you directly
or
indirectly choose to become."

CHOOSE WELL! ~ *lproctorm*

"Each of us has **POWER** and **INFLUENCE**. How we use it determines how powerful and influential we are." ~ *lproctorm*

"There are people you will be FRIENDS WITH and there are people you will to be <u>FRIENDS FOR Regardless...be the best friend you can be!"</u> ~ lproctorm

"The truth may hurt ONCE, A LIE hurts over and over…"

A lie…**FEARS** the truth

A lie…is **ASHAMED** of the truth

A lie…is **SELFISH**

A lie…is **SICK**

A lie…**AVOIDS** the truth

A lie…**ALWAYS** leads a trail to the truth.

~ lproctorm

"We do not LOVE without gaining more than we can afford to lose."

~ lproctorm

"We do not grieve without first LOVING!" ~ *lproctorm*

"Gratification requires participation."

~ *Iproctorm*

\

"Love is worth fighting for, if you are fighting for each other."

~ lproctorm

Share your LIFE Quote Here...